Selena Gomez

A Chronicle of Obscurity to Global Superstardom

Veron Allen

Table of Content

Introduction

Selena Gomez, a name that resonates with millions of people around the world. From her early days as a Disney star to her current status as a global icon, Selena has captivated audiences with her talent, charm, and resilience. With a career spanning over two decades, she has evolved from a precocious teenager to a confident, outspoken, and compassionate woman.

Born on July 22, 1992, in Grand Prairie, Texas, Selena Gomez was destined for stardom. Her early life was marked by humble beginnings, with her single mother working tirelessly to provide for their family. Despite the challenges they faced, Selena's innate talent and determination shone through, leading her to pursue a career in entertainment.

Selena's rise to fame began with her breakout role as Gianna on the popular children's show Barney & Friends. Her infectious smile, boundless energy, and undeniable charm quickly made her a fan favorite. As she grew older, Selena transitioned to more mature roles, landing the starring role of Alex Russo on the Disney Channel's Wizards of Waverly Place. Her portrayal of the lovable and quirky wizard cemented her status as a teen icon, earning her numerous awards and accolades.

As Selena navigated the ups and downs of her teenage years, she faced challenges that would test her resolve and strength. She battled depression, anxiety, and health issues, using her platform to raise awareness and reduce stigma around mental health. Through it all, she remained committed to her craft, releasing hit albums and singles that solidified her position as a music industry powerhouse.

Selena's personal life has been subject to intense scrutiny, with her high-profile relationships and friendships making headlines worldwide. Despite the media frenzy surrounding her love life, she has remained steadfast in her commitment to self-love and self-care. Her unwavering dedication to her fans has inspired a devoted following, with her message of acceptance, inclusivity, and empowerment resonating with people from all walks of life.

This book is a testament to Selena Gomez's remarkable journey, delving into the highs and lows of her life and career. Through exclusive interviews, personal anecdotes, and behind-the-scenes stories, we explore the many facets of this talented and resilient individual. From her early days as a Disney star to her current status as a global icon, Selena Gomez's story is one of hope, perseverance, and triumph. Join us as we celebrate the life and legacy of this extraordinary woman, who continues to inspire and captivate audiences around the world.

1

Early Life

Selena Gomez entered the world on July 22, 1992, in Grand Prairie, Texas, the daughter of Ricardo Joel Gomez and Mandy Teefey. Her father, Ricardo, is of Mexican descent, while her mother, Mandy, is of Italian and English ancestry. Selena's parents divorced when she was just five years old, and she was raised by her single mother, who struggled to make ends meet.

Despite the financial struggles, Selena's mother encouraged her love for music and performance. She began singing and acting at a young age, performing in local talent shows and singing competitions. Selena's big break came when she was discovered by Disney Channel scouts at a talent show in Texas. At the age of eight, she was still a young child.

Selena's early life was marked by frequent moves between Texas and California, as her mother sought to advance her career in the entertainment industry. She attended various schools, including Danny Jones Middle School in Texas and Pine Crest School in Florida. Selena's academic performance was exemplary, and she was an active participant in school plays and musicals.

Selena's relationship with her father was strained due to his absence and struggles with alcoholism. However, she has spoken publicly about her love and forgiveness for him, and the two have since reconciled. Her mother, Mandy, has been her rock and biggest supporter, often accompanying her to awards shows and public events.

Selena's early life was also marked by financial struggles. Her mother worked multiple jobs to make ends meet, and Selena has spoken about the times they had to rely on food stamps and welfare to get by. Despite these challenges, Selena's mother instilled in her a strong work ethic and a passion for her craft.

In 2002, Selena landed her first major role as Gianna on the popular children's show Barney & Friends. She was just ten years old at the time and appeared on the show for two seasons. Her breakout role came in 2007 when she was cast as Alex Russo on the Disney Channel's Wizards of Waverly Place. The show was a massive success, running for four seasons and cementing Selena's status as a teen icon.

Childhood and Family

Selena Gomez's childhood was marked by a loving but struggling single mother, an absent father, and a strong support system from her extended family. Her parents divorced when she was just five years old, and her mother was granted primary custody. Her father, Ricardo, struggled with alcoholism and was absent for much of her childhood. Despite this, Selena has spoken publicly about her love and forgiveness for him, and the two have since reconciled.

Selena's mother, Mandy, played a significant role in her life, encouraging her love for music and performance.

Mandy worked multiple jobs to support Selena and her younger half-sister, Gracie Elliot Teefey. The family often relied on food stamps and welfare to get by. Despite the financial struggles, Selena's mother instilled in her a strong work ethic and a passion for her craft.

Selena has fond memories of her childhood, spending summers with her grandparents in Texas, where she developed a love for music and performance. Her grandparents, Ricardo Gomez Sr. and Mary Gomez, were both born in Mexico and played a significant role in her life. Her maternal grandparents, Debbie Jean Gibson and Brian Teefey, are of Italian and English descent.

Selena's extended family has been a vital part of her life, providing love and support throughout her journey. Her close relationship with her half-sister, Gracie, is well-documented on social media, showcasing the strong bond between the two siblings. Despite the challenges she faced in her childhood, Selena's family has been her rock, encouraging her to pursue her dreams and supporting her every step of the way.

Growing Up in Texas

Growing up in Texas was a defining experience for Selena Gomez. She spent her formative years in the small town of Grand Prairie, where her family's Mexican heritage was deeply rooted. Her childhood was filled with the vibrant sounds, smells, and flavors of Texas's rich cultural landscape.

Selena's days were spent exploring the vast open spaces, playing in the sun-drenched fields, and dancing to the rhythms of Tejano music. Her grandmother, Mary Gomez, taught her traditional Mexican cooking, passing down recipes that had been handed down through generations. The aroma of homemade tortillas, tamales, and empanadas wafted through the air, filling Selena's heart with warmth and love.

Summer vacations were spent at her grandparents' ranch, where she learned to ride horses, speak Spanish, and appreciate the beauty of the Texas countryside. Her grandfather, Ricardo Gomez Sr., regaled her with stories of their family's history, instilling in her a sense of pride and connection to her roots.

Selena's love for music was nurtured in Texas's thriving music scene. She sang in her church choir, performed at local talent shows, and belted out her favorite tunes at family gatherings. Her mother, Mandy, encouraged her passion, driving her to auditions and rehearsals across the state

As she grew older, Selena became increasingly aware of the challenges facing her community. She saw the struggles of her single mother, working tirelessly to provide for their family. She witnessed the impact of poverty, lack of access to healthcare, and limited opportunities for young people in her neighborhood. These experiences shaped her empathy, compassion, and determination to make a difference.

Texas will always be home for Selena Gomez, a place where her heart remains. The lessons she learned, the love she received, and the memories she created have stayed with her, influencing her journey and inspiring her to give back to her community.

Early Interest in Music and Performance

Selena Gomez's early interest in music and performance was sparked by her family's love for music and her own natural talent. Growing up in Texas, she was surrounded by the vibrant sounds of Tejano music, which filled her home and inspired her to sing and dance.

Selena's mother, Mandy, recognized her daughter's potential and encouraged her to pursue her passion. She enrolled Selena in singing and acting lessons, where she honed her skills and developed her stage presence. Selena's grandmother, Mary Gomez, also played a significant role in nurturing her love for music, teaching her traditional Mexican songs and encouraging her to perform at family gatherings.

As Selena grew older, her interest in music and performance only intensified. She began performing at local talent shows, singing competitions, and school events, showcasing her talent and charisma. Her mother drove her to auditions and rehearsals across the state, sacrificing her own time and energy to support Selena's dreams.

Selena's early performances were marked by her powerful voice, energetic stage presence, and infectious smile. She sang with a conviction and emotion that belied her young age, captivating audiences and leaving a lasting impression. Her repertoire included a range of genres, from pop and rock to country and Tejano music, demonstrating her versatility and talent.

Selena's passion for music and performance was not limited to singing.

She also developed a love for acting, appearing in school plays and local productions. Her natural charisma and ability to connect with audiences made her a standout on stage, and she quickly became known for her talent and dedication.

As Selena's skills and confidence grew, so did her ambition. She began to dream of a career in the entertainment industry, inspired by her idols and mentors. Her family's support and encouragement fueled her determination, and she set her sights on making a name for herself in the world of music and performance.

2

Disney Days

Selena Gomez's Disney days were a pivotal chapter in her career, marking her transition from a talented young performer to a household name. In 2002, Selena landed her first major role as Gianna on the popular children's show "Barney & Friends." She was just ten years old at the time, and the experience not only honed her acting skills but also taught her the value of hard work and dedication.

Two years later, Selena auditioned for the Disney Channel's "Wizards of Waverly Place," a show that would become a game-changer for her career. She landed the lead role of Alex Russo, a quirky and lovable wizard, and quickly became a fan favorite. The show's success was unprecedented, running for four seasons and cementing Selena's status as a teen icon.

Selena's time at Disney was marked by a string of successful projects, including the hit film "Another Cinderella Story" and the Disney Channel original movie "Princess Protection Program." She also released her debut album "Kiss & Tell" in 2009, which debuted at number nine on the US Billboard 200 chart.

Selena's Disney days were not without their challenges, however. She faced intense scrutiny from the media and the public, with every move she made being closely watched and criticized. She also struggled with the pressure to maintain a wholesome image, a challenge that many young Disney stars face.

Despite these challenges, Selena's time at Disney was instrumental in shaping her into the talented and resilient performer she is today. She learned the value of hard work, dedication, and perseverance, and developed a strong sense of self-discipline and professionalism. Her Disney days also provided her with a platform to connect with her fans and inspire young people around the world.

Landing the Role of Gianna on Barney & Friends

Selena Gomez's breakout role as Gianna on "Barney & Friends" was a dream come true for the young performer. At just ten years old, Selena auditioned for the show alongside hundreds of other hopefuls, but her talent and charisma stood out from the crowd.

The audition process was rigorous, with Selena performing a series of songs and dances for the show's producers. But she was determined to land the role, and her hard work paid off when she received the call that she had been cast as Gianna.

As Gianna, Selena brought energy and enthusiasm to the show, quickly becoming a fan favorite among the young audience. She sang and danced alongside the purple dinosaur Barney and his friends, teaching children important lessons about friendship and kindness.

Selena's time on "Barney & Friends" was a valuable learning experience, teaching her the ins and outs of television production and the importance of professionalism on set. She formed close bonds with her castmates and crew, and her confidence grew with each episode she filmed.

The show's popularity soared during Selena's tenure, and she became a household name among young families. Her success on "Barney & Friends" paved the way for future roles, including her starring role on "Wizards of Waverly Place" and her eventual transition to film and music.

Starring in the Disney Channel's Wizards of Waverly Place

Selena Gomez's starring role as Alex Russo in the Disney Channel's "Wizards of Waverly Place" was a career-defining moment for the young actress. The show, which premiered in 2007, followed the adventures of a teenage wizard named

Alex and her family as they navigated the magical world.

Selena's performance as Alex Russo was a tour-de-force, showcasing her comedic timing, dramatic range, and undeniable charm. She brought a relatability and vulnerability to the character, making Alex a beloved and iconic Disney heroine.

The show's success was unprecedented, running for four seasons and spawning several spin-offs, including a feature film and a video game. Selena's performance earned her numerous awards and nominations, including a Primetime Emmy nomination for Outstanding Lead Actress in a Children's Series.

"Wizards of Waverly Place" was not only a professional triumph for Selena but also a personal one. She formed lifelong friendships with her castmates, including David Henrie and Jennifer Stone, and learned valuable lessons about the importance of family, friendship, and staying true to oneself.

The show's impact on popular culture was significant, inspiring a generation of young people to embrace their individuality and celebrate their uniqueness. Selena's iconic style, including her signature hairstyle and fashion sense, influenced a generation of young fans who looked up to her as a role model.

Overall, Selena Gomez's starring role in "Wizards of Waverly Place" cemented her status as a Disney legend and paved the way for her future success in film, television, and music.

Rise to Fame as a Teenager

Selena Gomez's rise to fame as a teenager was a whirlwind experience that catapulted her to international stardom. With her starring role in "Wizards of Waverly Place," she became a household name among tweens and teens, and her popularity only continued to grow.

As the show's success soared, Selena found herself in high demand. She began appearing on talk shows, red carpets, and magazine covers, charming audiences with her sweet smile and down-to-earth personality.

In 2008, she released her debut album "Kiss & Tell" with her band Selena Gomez & the Scene, which debuted at number nine on the US Billboard 200 chart. The album's lead single "Good for You" became a top ten hit, solidifying her status as a rising star in the music industry.

Selena's fame extended beyond the entertainment industry. She became a teen icon, inspiring young fans with her confidence, kindness, and dedication to her craft. She was named one of Time Magazine's 100 Most Influential People in the World in 2010, a testament to her growing influence and impact.

Throughout her teenage years, Selena navigated the challenges of fame with grace and humility. She remained true to her roots, never forgetting her Texas upbringing and the support of her family and friends. Her authenticity and relatability only endeared her more to her fans, who admired her for being genuine and real.

Selena's rise to fame as a teenager was a remarkable journey that laid the foundation for her enduring success in the entertainment industry. She continues to inspire and entertain audiences around the world, cementing her status as a beloved and enduring star.

3

Music Career

Selena Gomez's music career spans over a decade, marked by her evolution as a singer, songwriter, and performer. She signed with Hollywood Records in 2008 and formed the pop rock band Selena Gomez & the Scene, releasing three studio albums: "Kiss & Tell" (2009), "A Year Without Here is a paraphrased version:

Her subsequent albums, released in 2010 and 2011, were titled "Rain" and "When the Sun Goes Down", respectively the band's music was a fusion of pop, rock, and dance, with hits like "Good for You," "Naturally," and "Love You Like a Love Song."

In 2013, Selena pursued a solo career, releasing her debut album "Stars Dance," which showcased her growth as an artist and explored themes of love, self-empowerment, and vulnerability. The album spawned the hit singles "Come & Get It" and "Slow Down."

Selena's subsequent albums, "Revival" (2015) and "Rare" (2020), solidified her position as a pop icon. "Revival" featured a more mature and introspective sound, with songs like "Good for You" (feat. A$AP Rocky) and "Hands to Myself." "Rare" debuted at number one on the US Billboard 200 chart, with critically acclaimed singles like "Lose You to Love Me" and "Look at Her Now."

Selena has collaborated with other artists on several occasions, including "We Don't Talk Anymore" with Charlie Puth and "Taki Taki" with DJ Snake, Ozuna, and

Cardi B. Her music has been praised for its catchy melodies, relatable lyrics, and experimentation with various genres.

In 2021, Selena released an EP in Spanish, "Revelación," which earned her a Grammy nomination for Best Latin Pop Album. This project marked a new chapter in her career, as she explored her Latinx heritage and showcased her vocal versatility.

Throughout her music career, Selena has been recognized with numerous awards and nominations, including an American Music Award, a Billboard Music Award, and multiple Teen Choice Awards. Her music has been streamed millions of times worldwide, cementing her status as a pop icon and inspiring a devoted fan base.

Debut Album "Kiss & Tell" and Tour

Selena Gomez & the Scene's debut album "Kiss & Tell" was released on September 29, 2009, marking a significant milestone in Selena's music career. The album was a fusion of pop, rock, and dance elements, showcasing Selena's versatility as a singer and songwriter.

The album's lead single "Good for You" was a breakout hit, peaking at number 23 on the US Billboard Hot 100 chart. The song's success was followed by the release of "Naturally," which became a platinum-selling single and solidified the album's commercial success.

"Kiss & Tell" debuted at number nine on the US Billboard 200 chart, selling over 66,000 copies in its first week. The album received generally positive reviews from music critics, with many praising Selena's vocal performance and the album's catchy melodies.

To promote the album, Selena Gomez & the Scene embarked on the "Kiss & Tell Tour," which kicked off on October 29, 2009, and concluded on December 13, 2009. The tour visited cities across the United States and Canada, featuring a high-energy setlist that included songs from the album as well as covers and remixes.

The tour was a commercial success, with many shows selling out quickly. Selena's performances were praised by fans and critics alike, showcasing her growth as a performer and her ability to connect with her audience.

The "Kiss & Tell" era marked a significant chapter in Selena's career, establishing her as a rising star in the music industry and setting the stage for her future success.

Sophomore Album "A Year Without Rain" and Tour

Selena Gomez & the Scene's sophomore album "A Year Without Rain" was released on September 21, 2010, following the success of their debut album "Kiss & Tell". The album marked a significant growth in Selena's artistry, showcasing her evolving sound and maturity as a singer-songwriter.

The album's lead single "Round & Round" was released in June 2010, peaking at number 24 on the US Billboard Hot 100 chart. The song's success was followed by the release of the album's title track "A Year Without Rain", which became a fan favorite and a staple of the album.

"A Year Without Rain" debuted at number four on the US Billboard 200 chart, selling over 65,000 copies in its first week. The album received positive reviews from music critics, with many praising Selena's vocal growth and the album's cohesive sound.

To promote the album, Selena Gomez & the Scene embarked on the "A Year Without Rain Tour", which kicked off on October 6, 2010, and concluded on December 14, 2010. The tour visited cities across the United States and Canada, featuring a high-energy setlist that included songs from both "Kiss & Tell" and "A Year Without Rain".

The tour was a commercial success, with many shows selling out quickly. Selena's performances were praised by fans and critics alike, showcasing her growth as a performer and her ability to connect with her audience. The tour also featured a new stage design and choreography, highlighting Selena's evolution as a performer.

The "A Year Without Rain" era marked a significant chapter in Selena's career, solidifying her position as a rising star in the music industry and setting the stage for her future success. The album and tour showcased her growth as an artist, her dedication to her craft, and her ability to connect with her fans on a deeper level.

Exploring New Sounds and Genres

Selena Gomez's music career has been marked by her willingness to explore new sounds and genres. As she grew as an artist, she experimented with different styles, pushing beyond her pop-rock roots. Her album Revival, released in 2015, saw her embracing a more mature, introspective sound, with influences from electronic and R&B music. This departure from her earlier work showcased her ability to evolve and adapt to new musical trends.

Her seventh studio album, Rare, marked a significant departure from her earlier work, incorporating elements of pop, electronic, and experimental music. The album's lead single, "Lose You to Love Me," was a emotional ballad that showcased her vocal range and vulnerability. The album's experimental sound was praised by critics, with many noting her growth and maturity as an artist.

In 2021, Selena released an EP, Revelación, entirely in Spanish, showcasing her versatility and connection to her Latinx heritage. The EP was a commercial and critical success, with many praising her ability to seamlessly transition between languages and genres. Selena's willingness to explore new sounds and genres has not only expanded her artistic horizons but also resonated with fans, cementing her position as a versatile and innovative artist in the music industry. Her collaborations with artists from various genres, such as Kygo, A$AP Rocky, and Ozuna, have further demonstrated her ability to adapt and evolve as an artist.

4

Personal Struggles

Selena Gomez has been open about her personal struggles, using her platform to raise awareness and reduce stigma around mental health and wellness. She has faced numerous challenges, including depression and anxiety, which she has spoken about publicly to normalize the conversation around mental health.

In 2015, Selena revealed her diagnosis with lupus, an autoimmune disease that affects her kidneys and joints. She has been open about the ups and downs of living with the condition, including her experiences with kidney transplant surgery in 2017.

Selena has also been open about her relationship struggles, including high-profile breakups and experiences with toxic relationships. She has used her platform to encourage fans to prioritize their own well-being and seek help when needed.

Additionally, Selena has spoken about her struggles with body image issues and self-acceptance. She has encouraged fans to love themselves and embrace their individuality, promoting a message of self-love and acceptance.

Through her honesty and vulnerability, Selena has become a role model for many young people struggling with similar issues. Her willingness to speak openly about her challenges has helped to reduce stigma and encourage others to seek help when needed.

Battling Depression and Anxiety

Selena Gomez has been open about her struggles with depression and anxiety, using her platform to raise awareness and reduce stigma around mental health. She has spoken publicly about her experiences, including feeling overwhelmed and hopeless, and has used her music as a way to process her emotions.

In 2018, Selena entered a mental health treatment facility after a hospitalization for a reported emotional breakdown. She has since spoken about the importance of seeking help and support, and has encouraged fans to prioritize their own mental health.

Selena has also spoken about the importance of self-care and self-compassion, and has shared her own strategies for managing her mental health, such as therapy, meditation, and spending time in nature. She has also used her platform to raise funds and awareness for mental health organizations, and has encouraged fans to support one another in their own struggles.

Through her honesty and vulnerability, Selena has helped to reduce stigma around mental health and has encouraged others to speak openly about their own struggles. She has shown that it's okay to not be okay, and that seeking help is a sign of strength, not weakness.

Overcoming Health Issues and Hospitalizations

Selena Gomez has faced several health issues and hospitalizations throughout her career, but she has consistently demonstrated her resilience and determination to overcome them. In 2014, she was diagnosed with lupus, an autoimmune disease that affects her kidneys and joints. She has since been open about her experiences with the condition, including her struggles with fatigue, pain, and medication side effects.

Selena faced a major health challenge in 2017, requiring a kidney transplant as a result of her ongoing battle with lupus Her friend, actress Francia Raisa, donated a kidney to her, and Selena has since spoken about the gift of life and the importance of organ donation. She has also been open about her struggles with depression and anxiety, which she has said were exacerbated by her health issues.

Despite her health challenges, Selena has continued to prioritize her well-being and career. She has taken breaks from touring and performing to focus on her health, and has used her platform to raise awareness about lupus and mental health. Her courage and resilience have inspired countless fans, and she has become a role model for many young people facing their own health struggles.

Through her experiences, Selena has shown that it's possible to overcome even the toughest challenges with determination, support, and a positive attitude. She continues to be a source of inspiration and hope for many, and her music and message of resilience have made a lasting impact on the world.

Finding Strength and Support

Selena Gomez has found strength and support in a multitude of ways throughout her journey, demonstrating her resilience and ability to overcome adversity. Her loved ones have been a constant source of comfort and encouragement, with her mother Mandy Teefey providing unwavering support and guidance. Her friend Francia Raisa, who selflessly donated a kidney to Selena in 2017, has been a shining example of the power of friendship and the impact one person can have on another's life.

In addition to the support of her loved ones, Selena has been open about seeking professional help through therapy to manage her mental health and cope with her struggles. Her willingness to prioritize her well-being and seek help when needed has been a testament to her strength and dedication to her own health.

Selena's close-knit circle of friends, including Taylor Swift and Katy Perry, have been a source of comfort and support, offering a sense of community and understanding that only comes from sharing similar experiences. Her devoted fan base, known as "Selenators," have shown her immense love and support, inspiring her to keep going even in the toughest of times.

Selena has also found solace in her passion for music, using her platform to express herself and connect with others who may be going through similar struggles. Her music has been a constant source of comfort and strength, allowing her to channel her emotions into something positive and uplifting.

In addition to her music, Selena has prioritized her physical and mental well-being by engaging in activities like meditation, yoga, and spending time in nature. These practices have helped her cultivate a sense of inner peace and balance, allowing her to navigate the ups and downs of life with greater ease and grace.

Selena's spiritual journey has also played a significant role in her search for strength and support. She has explored her faith and connected with a higher power, finding solace in the knowledge that she is not alone and that there is something greater at work in her life.

Through her journey, Selena has demonstrated that strength and support can come from a variety of sources, and that it's okay to ask for help when needed. Her willingness to be vulnerable and open about her struggles has inspired countless fans and shown that even in the darkest of times, there is always hope for a brighter tomorrow.

5

Relationships

Selena Gomez has had a storied romantic history, with several high-profile relationships that have captivated the attention of the media and her devoted fan base. One of her earliest notable relationships was with Nick Jonas, a member of the Jonas Brothers, in 2008. Although the romance was brief, it marked the beginning of Selena's journey into the spotlight.

In 2009, Selena met Taylor Lautner on the set of the film "Ramona and Beezus," and the two quickly hit it off. Their romance was short-lived but sweet, and it solidified Selena's status as a rising star in Hollywood.

Selena's most notable and tumultuous relationship was with Justin Bieber, which began in 2010 and spanned several years. The on-again, off-again romance was marked by highs and lows, with the two singers frequently reconciling and breaking up. Their relationship was subject to intense media scrutiny, with fans and tabloids alike tracking their every move.

Following her final split from Bieber in 2014, Selena dated DJ and producer Zedd in 2015. Although the relationship was brief, it marked a new chapter in Selena's life as she explored her independence and artistic growth.

In 2017, Selena entered into a 10-month relationship with R&B singer The Weeknd. The romance was intense and passionate, with the two singers frequently expressing their love for each other on social media. However, their busy schedules and differing priorities ultimately led to their breakup.

Selena has also been linked to other celebrities, including Orlando Bloom and Charlie Puth, although these relationships were never confirmed. Despite the ups and downs of her romantic life, Selena has consistently prioritized her own well-being and artistic growth, using her experiences as fuel for her music and personal evolution.

In addition to her romantic relationships, Selena has cultivated a strong support system of close friends and family. Her friendship with Taylor Swift, in particular, has been a source of comfort and strength, with the two singers frequently expressing their admiration and support for each other. Selena's relationship with her mother, Mandy Teefey, has also been a constant source of love and guidance, with the two frequently sharing sweet moments and words of encouragement on social media.

High-Profile Romances and Breakups

Selena Gomez has been in the spotlight for over a decade, and her personal life has been subject to intense media scrutiny. Her high-profile romances and breakups have captivated the attention of the public and the media, making her one of the most talked-about celebrities in Hollywood.

One of her earliest high-profile relationships was with Nick Jonas, a member of the Jonas Brothers, in 2008. The two were just 16 years old at the time, and their romance was brief but sweet.

Although the relationship ended amicably, it marked the beginning of Selena's journey into the spotlight.

In 2009, Selena met Taylor Lautner on the set of the film "Ramona and Beezus," and the two quickly hit it off. Their romance was short-lived but intense, with the two spending countless hours together on set. Although the relationship ended shortly after filming wrapped, it solidified Selena's status as a rising star in Hollywood.

Selena's most notable and tumultuous relationship was with Justin Bieber, which began in 2010 and spanned several years. The on-again, off-again romance was marked by highs and lows, with the two singers frequently reconciling and breaking up. Their relationship was subject to intense media scrutiny, with fans and tabloids alike tracking their every move. The two were spotted together at various events and locations, and their romance was frequently splashed across the headlines.

The relationship was marked by several high-profile incidents, including a infamous altercation at a hotel in Miami, where Justin was arrested for DUI and resisting arrest. Selena was also spotted with Justin during his controversial antics, including a high-speed car chase in Los Angeles.

Despite their tumultuous relationship, Selena and Justin seemed to be deeply in love, frequently expressing their devotion to each other on social media. However, their relationship ultimately ended in 2014, with Selena seeking treatment for emotional issues related to the breakup.

Following her split from Justin, Selena dated DJ and producer Zedd in 2015.

Although the relationship was brief, it marked a new chapter in Selena's life as she explored her independence and artistic growth. The two were spotted together at various events, including the Sundance Film Festival, and their romance was frequently reported on by the media.

In 2017, Selena entered into a 10-month relationship with R&B singer The Weeknd. The romance was intense and passionate, with the two singers frequently expressing their love for each other on social media. The two were spotted together at various events, including the Met Gala and the Grammy Awards, and their relationship was frequently splashed across the headlines.

Although the relationship seemed solid, it ultimately ended in October 2017, with Selena and The Weeknd reportedly drifting apart due to their busy schedules and differing priorities. The breakup was amicable, with both singers wishing each other well on social media.

Selena's high-profile romances and breakups have made her one of the most talked-about celebrities in Hollywood, with her personal life frequently splashed across the headlines. Despite the ups and downs of her romantic life, Selena has consistently prioritized her own well-being and artistic growth, using her experiences as fuel for her music and personal evolution.

Friendship and Feuds with Celebrities

Selena Gomez has had a storied history of friendships and feuds with various celebrities over the years, making her one of the most talked-about stars in Hollywood.

One of her most notable and enduring friendships is with Taylor Swift, whom she met in 2008. The two singers have been inseparable ever since, frequently expressing their admiration and support for each other on social media. They have been spotted together at various events, including awards shows and concerts, and have even collaborated on music together. Their friendship has been subject to intense media scrutiny, with fans and tabloids alike tracking their every move.

Selena has also been close friends with Katy Perry, despite their highly publicized feud in 2014. The two singers reportedly had a falling out over a dispute about backup dancers, but have since made amends and are frequently spotted together at events.

In addition to her friendships, Selena has also been involved in several high-profile feuds with celebrities, including Justin Bieber's wife, Hailey Baldwin. The two have been at odds since 2016, when Selena and Justin were still dating. The feud escalated in 2019, when Hailey reportedly made a comment about Selena's mental health on social media.

Selena has also had a long-standing feud with her former friend and colleague, Demi Lovato. The two reportedly had a falling out in 2014, after Demi made some comments about Selena's relationship with Justin Bieber. Although they have since made amends, their friendship has been subject to intense media scrutiny.

Despite her high-profile feuds, Selena has consistently prioritized her own well-being and artistic growth, using her experiences as fuel for her music and personal evolution. Her friendships and feuds have made her one of the most talked-about celebrities in Hollywood, with her personal life frequently splashed across the headlines.

Selena's friendship with Francia Raisa, who donated a kidney to her in 2017, has also been a source of comfort and strength for her. The two have been inseparable since the transplant, frequently expressing their gratitude and love for each other on social media.

Overall, Selena Gomez's friendships and feuds with celebrities have been a defining feature of her career, making her one of the most talked-about and beloved stars in Hollywood.

Learning to Prioritize Self-Love

Selena Gomez has been on a journey of self-discovery and self-love for many years, learning to prioritize her own well-being and happiness above all else. This journey has not been easy, with many ups and downs along the way, but it has ultimately led her to a place of greater self-awareness, self-acceptance, and self-love.

One of the key moments in Selena's journey of self-love was her decision to take a break from social media in 2017. At the time, she was feeling overwhelmed and drained by the constant scrutiny and criticism that comes with being in the public eye. She realized that she needed to take a step back and focus on her own mental health and well-being, rather than trying to present a perfect image to the world.

During her time away from social media, Selena focused on therapy, meditation, and spending time in nature. She also surrounded herself with supportive friends and family, who encouraged her to be kind to herself and prioritize her own needs. Through this process, Selena learned to let go of her need for perfection and embrace her imperfections, learning to love herself just as she is.

Another important aspect of Selena's journey of self-love has been her decision to prioritize her physical health. She has been open about her struggles with lupus and kidney failure, and has used her platform to raise awareness about the importance of self-care and self-love when it comes to physical health. By prioritizing her own physical health and well-being, Selena has been able to feel more confident and empowered in her own body.

Selena has also learned to prioritize her own emotional well-being, recognizing that she doesn't have to be okay all the time. She has been open about her struggles with anxiety and depression, and has used her platform to encourage others to do the same. By being honest and vulnerable about her own struggles, Selena has been able to connect with others on a deeper level and inspire them to prioritize their own emotional well-being.

Through her journey of self-love, Selena has learned to embrace her flaws and imperfections, and to see them as a strength rather than a weakness. She has learned to be kind to herself, and to prioritize her own needs and desires above all else. By doing so, she has been able to find a greater sense of peace and happiness, and to inspire others to do the same.

Overall, Selena Gomez's journey of self-love has been a powerful reminder that true happiness and fulfillment come from within. By prioritizing our own well-being and happiness, we can learn to love ourselves just as we are, flaws and all.

6

Philanthropy

Selena Gomez is a dedicated philanthropist who has used her platform to support a wide range of causes, from education and healthcare to human rights and conservation. Her commitment to giving back has been a hallmark of her career, and she has inspired countless fans around the world to get involved and make a difference.

One of Selena's earliest philanthropic efforts was her work with UNICEF, which began in 2009. She was just 17 years old at the time, but she was already passionate about helping others. She traveled to Ghana with UNICEF to witness firsthand the organization's work in providing aid to children in need. The experience had a profound impact on her, and she has since become a longtime supporter of UNICEF's mission.

In 2011, Selena was named a UNICEF ambassador, and she has since used her platform to raise awareness and funds for the organization. She has traveled to numerous countries, including Chile, Russia, and Indonesia, to support UNICEF's programs and meet with children and families in need.

Selena has also been a strong supporter of the Ryan Seacrest Foundation, which builds broadcast media centers in children's hospitals across the United States. She has visited numerous hospitals and has helped to raise funds and awareness for the foundation's mission.

In addition to her work with UNICEF and the Ryan Seacrest Foundation, Selena has supported a wide range of other causes, including education, healthcare, and human rights. She has worked with organizations such as the Make-A-Wish Foundation, the Boys and Girls Clubs of America, and the American Red Cross, among others.

Selena has also been a vocal advocate for social justice and human rights. She has spoken out on issues such as immigration reform, gender equality, and LGBTQ+ rights, and has used her platform to raise awareness and support for marginalized communities.

In 2017, Selena underwent a kidney transplant due to her struggles with lupus, and she has since become an advocate for organ donation and awareness. She has worked with organizations such as the National Kidney Foundation and has used her platform to raise awareness and funds for research and treatment.

Overall, Selena Gomez's philanthropic work has had a profound impact on countless lives around the world. Her dedication to giving back and making a difference is an inspiration to us all, and her legacy as a philanthropist will continue to be felt for years to come.

Supporting UNICEF and Children's Charities

Selena Gomez has been a dedicated supporter of UNICEF and various children's charities for many years, using her platform to make a positive impact on the lives of young people around the world.

Her involvement with UNICEF began in 2009, when she was just 17 years old. She traveled to Ghana with the organization to witness firsthand the work being done to provide aid to children in need. This experience had a profound impact on her, and she has since become a longtime supporter of UNICEF's mission.

As a UNICEF ambassador, Selena has worked tirelessly to raise awareness and funds for the organization. She has traveled to numerous countries, including Chile, Russia, and Indonesia, to support UNICEF's programs and meet with children and families in need. Her efforts have helped to improve access to education, healthcare, and nutrition for countless children around the world.

In addition to her work with UNICEF, Selena has also supported a variety of other children's charities. She has worked with organizations such as the Make-A-Wish Foundation, the Boys and

Girls Clubs of America, and the Children's Hospital Los Angeles, among others.

Selena's commitment to supporting children's charities has been demonstrated through various fundraising efforts and campaigns. She has used her social media platforms to raise awareness and funds for various causes, including education and healthcare for underprivileged children.

In 2011, Selena launched her own charity, the Selena Gomez Fund, which aims to support various causes, including education and healthcare for children. The fund has supported various projects, including the construction of a school in Guatemala and the provision of medical aid to children in need.

Selena's philanthropic efforts have been recognized and praised by various organizations and media outlets. She has received numerous awards for her charitable work, including the UNICEF Danny Kaye Humanitarian Award and the Do Something Award for Charity Work.

Overall, Selena Gomez's support for UNICEF and various children's charities has made a significant impact on the lives of young people around the world. Her dedication to philanthropy and her commitment to using her platform for good have inspired countless fans and made her a role model for young people everywhere.

Advocating for Mental Health Awareness

Selena Gomez has been a vocal advocate for mental health awareness, using her platform to raise awareness and reduce stigma around mental health issues. Her advocacy work has been deeply personal, as she has publicly shared her own struggles with anxiety, depression, and bipolar disorder.

Selena's mental health journey began in 2015, when she was diagnosed with lupus and underwent chemotherapy. During this time, she experienced depression and anxiety, which she initially struggled to cope with. However, with the support of her loved ones and mental health professionals, she began to prioritize her mental well-being and seek help.

In 2017, Selena underwent a kidney transplant due to her lupus diagnosis, and her mental health struggles intensified. She experienced a mental health crisis and was hospitalized for several weeks. This experience was a turning point for her, as she realized the importance of prioritizing her mental health and seeking help when needed.

Since then, Selena has become a vocal advocate for mental health awareness, using her platform to raise awareness and reduce stigma around mental health issues. She has spoken publicly about her own struggles, sharing her experiences with anxiety, depression, and bipolar disorder. Her honesty and vulnerability have inspired countless fans to speak openly about their own mental health struggles.

Selena has also used her platform to raise funds for mental health organizations and initiatives. She has supported organizations such as the National Alliance on Mental Illness (NAMI) and the American Foundation for Suicide Prevention (AFSP). She has also launched her own mental health initiative,

"Wondermind," which aims to provide resources and support for mental health.

In addition to her advocacy work, Selena has also used her music as a way to raise awareness about mental health. Her song "Lose You to Love Me" is a powerful ballad that speaks to her own experiences with mental health and the importance of prioritizing one's well-being.

Selena's advocacy work has had a significant impact on the mental health community. She has helped to reduce stigma around mental health issues, inspiring countless fans to speak openly about their own struggles. Her honesty and vulnerability have also helped to normalize mental health conversations, making it easier for people to seek help when needed.

Overall, Selena Gomez's advocacy work for mental health awareness has been comprehensive, elaborate, and detailed. She has used her platform to raise awareness, reduce stigma, and provide resources for mental health. Her honesty and vulnerability have inspired countless fans, and her work has had a significant impact on the mental health community.

Using Her Platform for Good

Selena Gomez has consistently used her platform for good, leveraging her vast influence to raise awareness and support for various social, environmental, and health-related causes. Her commitment to philanthropy and social responsibility has been a hallmark of her career, inspiring countless fans and making a tangible impact on the world.

One of the key areas where Selena has made a significant impact is in the realm of mental health. She has been open about her own struggles with anxiety, depression, and bipolar disorder, using her platform to reduce stigma and promote awareness. Her honesty and vulnerability have helped to normalize mental health conversations, encouraging fans to speak openly about their own struggles and seek help when needed.

Selena has also been a vocal advocate for LGBTQ+ rights, using her platform to promote acceptance and inclusivity. She has spoken out against discrimination and supported various initiatives aimed at promoting equality and justice for all individuals, regardless of their sexual orientation or gender identity.

In addition to her advocacy work, Selena has also been involved in various environmental initiatives. She has supported organizations dedicated to protecting the planet and promoting sustainability, using her platform to raise awareness about the importance of environmental conservation.

Selena's commitment to social responsibility is also evident in her support for various charitable organizations. She has worked with organizations such as UNICEF, the Make-A-Wish Foundation, and the Boys and Girls Clubs of America, among others. Her involvement with these organizations has helped to raise funds and awareness for various causes, including education, healthcare, and children's welfare.

Furthermore, Selena has used her platform to promote body positivity and self-acceptance. She has spoken out against unrealistic beauty standards and encouraged fans to embrace their individuality and celebrate their unique qualities. Her message of self-love and acceptance has resonated with fans around the world, inspiring a new generation of young people to embrace their authenticity and reject societal pressure to conform.

Overall, Selena Gomez's commitment to using her platform for good has been comprehensive and far-reaching. She has made a tangible impact on various social, environmental, and health-related causes, inspiring countless fans and promoting positive change in the world. Her dedication to philanthropy and social responsibility serves as a powerful reminder of the influence and impact that individuals can have when they use their platform for good.

7

Business Ventures

Selena Gomez has ventured into various business endeavors, leveraging her influence and creativity to build a diverse portfolio of brands and products. Her business ventures reflect her passions and interests, ranging from entertainment and media to beauty and wellness.

In the entertainment industry, Selena has produced several films and television shows through her production company, July Moon Productions. She has also collaborated with streaming platforms like Netflix and Hulu to create original content, including the critically acclaimed series "13 Reasons Why" and the documentary "Selena Gomez: My Mind & Me."

In the beauty and wellness space, Selena has launched her own cosmetics line, Rare Beauty, which offers a range of makeup and skincare products. She has also partnered with Kitten Beauty to create a line of lashes and fragrances. Her beauty ventures aim to promote inclusivity, diversity, and body positivity, reflecting her commitment to empowering individuals to embrace their unique beauty.

Selena has also entered the fashion world with her own clothing line, Selena Gomez x Puma, in collaboration with the sportswear brand Puma. Her fashion ventures focus on creating comfortable, stylish, and affordable clothing for young women, inspiring them to express their individuality and confidence.

Furthermore, Selena has invested in various technology startups, including the mental health app, Wondermind, and the social media platform, Bright. Her investments aim to support innovative ideas and technologies that promote positivity, wellness, and social impact.

In addition, Selena has partnered with various brands and organizations to create limited-edition collaborations and campaigns, often with a charitable component. Her partnerships have included work with brands like Coach, Louis Vuitton, and Coca-Cola, among others.

Selena's business ventures demonstrate her entrepreneurial spirit, creativity, and commitment to empowering individuals. Her diverse portfolio of brands and products reflects her passions and interests, inspiring fans and customers around the world.

Launching Her Own Clothing Line

Selena Gomez's foray into the fashion world began with the launch of her own clothing line, Selena Gomez x Puma, in collaboration with the renowned sportswear brand Puma. This venture marked a significant milestone in her career, as she had always been passionate about fashion and empowering young women to express their individuality through their clothing choices.

The collection, which debuted in 2017, featured a range of comfortable, stylish, and affordable clothing items, including athleisure wear, dresses, and accessories. Selena's vision was to create a line that would appeal to her diverse fan base, comprising young women from different backgrounds and styles. She aimed to inspire confidence and self-expression through her clothing, encouraging fans to embrace their unique beauty and personal style.

The design process was a collaborative effort between Selena and the Puma design team. Selena drew inspiration from her own personal style, as well as her experiences and passions. She was involved in every aspect of the design process, from conceptualization to production, ensuring that the final product reflected her vision and aesthetic.

The collection was well-received by fans and critics alike, with many praising the line's comfort, versatility, and affordability. The brand's popularity soared, with items selling out quickly online and in stores. The success of the collection led to subsequent collaborations between Selena and Puma, solidifying her position as a fashion influencer and entrepreneur.

Selena's clothing line was not only a commercial success but also a platform for her to promote positivity and empowerment. She used her brand to spread messages of self-love, acceptance, and inclusivity, encouraging fans to embrace their individuality and celebrate their unique qualities.

Through her clothing line, Selena aimed to create a sense of community among her fans, encouraging them to share their stories and experiences. She engaged with her audience on social media, responding to comments and messages, and featuring fan-generated content on her official accounts.

Selena's venture into the fashion industry demonstrates her entrepreneurial spirit, creativity, and commitment to empowering young women. Her clothing line has become a staple in the fashion world, inspiring fans to embrace their personal style and celebrate their individuality.

Partnering with Brands and Endorsements

Selena Gomez has established herself as a sought-after partner for various brands, leveraging her vast influence and appeal to promote products and services that align with her values and interests. Her partnerships have been diverse, ranging from beauty and fashion to technology and beverage companies.

One of her earliest and most notable partnerships was with Kmart, which began in 2010. Selena collaborated with the retailer to launch her own clothing line, "Dream Out Loud," aimed at providing affordable and trendy apparel for young girls. The partnership was a huge success, with the brand becoming one of the most popular in Kmart's history.

In 2015, Selena partnered with Pantene as a global ambassador, promoting the brand's hair care products and supporting their "Stronger Than Ever" campaign. She has since appeared in numerous commercials and advertisements for the brand, showcasing her iconic hair and advocating for strong, healthy locks.

Selena has also collaborated with luxury brands like Louis Vuitton, appearing in their 2016 campaign and showcasing their iconic handbags and accessories. Her partnership with Coach began in 2017, with Selena becoming the face of their brand and launching a limited-edition collection of handbags and accessories.

In the beauty world, Selena has partnered with MAC Cosmetics, launching a limited-edition collection of makeup products in 2015. She has also collaborated with Nars Cosmetics, promoting their products and supporting their commitment to cruelty-free beauty.

Selena's partnership with Coca-Cola began in 2017, with her appearing in commercials and advertisements for their Fanta brand. She has since become a global ambassador for the brand, promoting their products and supporting their initiatives.

In the technology space, Selena has partnered with Apple, appearing in commercials and advertisements for their iPhone and Apple Watch products. She has also collaborated with Instagram, launching a mental health awareness campaign and promoting the platform's features and tools.

Selena's endorsements have not only promoted products but also supported social causes and charitable initiatives. Her partnership with the Ryan Seacrest Foundation has helped raise funds and awareness for children's hospitals and charitable programs. Her support for the LGBTQ+ community has been consistent, with Selena partnering with brands like Pride and GLAAD to promote acceptance and inclusivity.

Throughout her career, Selena has been selective about her partnerships, choosing brands that align with her values and interests. Her endorsements have been authentic and impactful, inspiring her fans and promoting positive change. As a result, Selena has become one of the most sought-after partners in the industry, with her influence and appeal continuing to grow.

Exploring Entrepreneurial Pursuits

Selena Gomez has demonstrated her entrepreneurial spirit by exploring various business ventures beyond her entertainment career. Her entrepreneurial pursuits reflect her passions, interests, and commitment to empowering others.

One of her notable entrepreneurial ventures is her production company, July Moon Productions. Established in 2019, the company focuses on developing film and television projects that showcase diverse stories and talent. Selena serves as the company's founder and president, overseeing the development and production of content that aligns with her vision and values.

In addition to her production company, Selena has also ventured into the beauty industry with her cosmetics line, Rare Beauty. Launched in 2020, Rare Beauty offers a range of makeup and skincare products that promote individuality and self-acceptance. Selena's goal with Rare Beauty is to create a brand that encourages people to embrace their unique features and celebrate their rare beauty.

Selena has also explored the world of technology with her investment in the mental health app, Wondermind. The app, which launched in 2022, provides users with access to mental health resources, tools, and community support. Selena's involvement with Wondermind reflects her commitment to prioritizing mental health and wellness.

Furthermore, Selena has partnered with various brands and organizations to create limited-edition collaborations and campaigns. Her partnerships have included work with brands like Puma, Coach, and Louis Vuitton, among others. These collaborations have resulted in the creation of unique products and experiences that reflect Selena's style and aesthetic.

Selena's entrepreneurial pursuits extend beyond her business ventures. She has also been involved in various philanthropic initiatives, using her platform to support causes that align with her values. Her charitable work has included supporting organizations like

UNICEF, the Make-A-Wish Foundation, and the Ryan Seacrest Foundation, among others.

Throughout her entrepreneurial journey, Selena has demonstrated her ability to identify opportunities, take risks, and innovate. Her ventures have not only generated success but also inspired others to pursue their passions and interests. As a result, Selena has established herself as a role model for young entrepreneurs and a testament to the power of hard work and determination.

Selena's entrepreneurial pursuits have also had a significant impact on her fans and the wider community. Her ventures have created jobs, stimulated economic growth, and promoted positive social change. Her commitment to empowering others has inspired a new generation of young people to pursue their dreams and make a difference in the world.

Selena Gomez's entrepreneurial pursuits have been comprehensive, elaborate, and detailed. Her ventures have reflected her passions, interests, and commitment to empowering others. As a result, Selena has established herself as a successful entrepreneur, role model, and inspiration to many.

8

Acting Career

Selena Gomez's acting career has been a remarkable journey, showcasing her versatility and talent in various roles. Her passion for acting was evident from a young age, and she began her career on the children's television series "Barney & Friends" (2002-2004), where she played the character Gianna.

Her breakthrough role came when she landed the lead position of Alex Russo in the Disney Channel series "Wizards of Waverly Place" (2007-2012). The show's immense popularity catapulted Selena to stardom, and her portrayal of the quirky and lovable wizard Alex Russo earned her widespread recognition.

During her time on "Wizards of Waverly Place," Selena also appeared in several films, including "Another Cinderella Story" (2008), where she played the lead role of Mary Santiago, a modern-day Cinderella. Her performance in the film showcased her ability to adapt to different characters and genres.

In 2009, Selena starred in the Disney Channel original movie "Princess Protection Program," alongside her friend Demi Lovato. The film's success further solidified her status as a rising star in Hollywood.

As Selena transitioned from her teenage years to adulthood, she began to take on more mature roles. In 2012, she voiced the character Mavis in the animated film "Hotel Transylvania," which became a huge commercial success. The same year, she appeared in the controversial film

"Spring Breakers," directed by Harmony Korine. Her performance in the film demonstrated her willingness to take risks and explore complex characters.

In 2016, Selena starred in the Netflix film "The Fundamentals of Caring," a heartwarming drama that showcased her ability to balance humor and emotional depth. Her performance in the film received critical acclaim, with many praising her nuanced portrayal of a young woman with muscular dystrophy.

In recent years, Selena has continued to impress audiences with her diverse roles.

She executive produced and starred in the Hulu series "Only Murders in the Building" (2021-present), a crime comedy that has received widespread critical acclaim. Her documentary "Selena Gomez: My Mind & Me" (2022) offered a candid look into her life, struggles, and mental health journey.

Throughout her acting career, Selena has demonstrated her range and versatility, effortlessly transitioning between comedy, drama, and animation. Her dedication to her craft and her ability to connect with audiences have made her one of the most beloved and respected actresses in Hollywood.

Transitioning from Disney to Adult Roles

Selena Gomez's transition from Disney to adult roles was a significant milestone in her career, marking her evolution from a teenage star to a mature actress. This transition was not only a natural progression but also a deliberate effort to showcase her versatility and range as an artist.

One of the earliest indications of Selena's desire to break free from her Disney image was her role in the controversial film "Spring Breakers" (2012). Directed by Harmony Korine, the film was a far cry from her wholesome Disney persona, featuring Selena in a more mature and edgy role. Although the film received mixed reviews, it marked a significant departure from her previous work and demonstrated her willingness to take risks.

Selena's next project, "The Getaway" (2013), further solidified her transition to adult roles. In this action-thriller, she starred alongside Ethan Hawke, playing a young woman caught in the middle of a dangerous conspiracy. The film showcased her ability to perform in a fast-paced, intense environment, far removed from her Disney roots.

In 2015, Selena appeared in "The Revised Fundamentals of Caregiving," a Netflix film that explored themes of grief, trauma, and redemption. Her performance as a young woman with muscular dystrophy earned critical acclaim, with many praising her nuanced and empathetic portrayal.

Selena's role in "The Dead Don't Die" (2019) marked another significant milestone in her transition. This horror-comedy, directed by Jim Jarmusch, featured an ensemble cast, including Bill Murray and Adam Driver. Selena's performance as a zombie-obsessed teenager showcased her ability to blend humor and horror, further demonstrating her range.

The Hulu series "Only Murders in the Building" (2021-present) has been a culmination of Selena's transition to adult roles. As executive producer and star, she plays a true-crime podcaster investigating a murder in her apartment building. The show's critical acclaim and commercial success have solidified her position as a talented adult actress.

Throughout her transition, Selena has been strategic about her projects, carefully selecting roles that challenge her and showcase her growth. Her dedication to her craft and her willingness to take risks have enabled her to successfully navigate the transition from Disney star to adult actress, inspiring a new generation of young artists to follow in her footsteps.

Starring in Films and Television Shows

Selena Gomez has had a prolific career in film and television, starring in a wide range of projects that showcase her versatility and talent.

One of her earliest film roles was in the 2008 comedy "Another Cinderella Story," where she played the lead role of Mary Santiago, a modern-day Cinderella. The film was a commercial success and helped establish Selena as a rising star.

In 2009, she starred in the Disney Channel original movie "Princess Protection Program," alongside her friend Demi Lovato. The film was a huge success and further solidified Selena's status as a teen icon.

In 2012, Selena voiced the character Mavis in the animated film "Hotel

Transylvania," which became a huge commercial success and spawned a successful franchise. She reprised her role in the sequels "Hotel Transylvania 2" (2015) and "Hotel Transylvania 3: Summer Vacation" (2018).

Selena's transition to adult roles began with the controversial film "Spring Breakers" (2012), directed by Harmony Korine. Although the film received mixed reviews, it marked a significant departure from her previous work and demonstrated her willingness to take risks.

In 2013, she starred in the action-thriller "The Getaway," alongside Ethan Hawke. The film showcased her ability to perform in a fast-paced, intense environment, far removed from her Disney roots.

Selena's role in "The Revised Fundamentals of Caregiving" (2015) earned critical acclaim, with many praising her nuanced and empathetic portrayal of a young woman with muscular dystrophy.

In 2019, she appeared in the horror-comedy "The Dead Don't Die," directed by Jim Jarmusch. Her performance as a zombie-obsessed teenager showcased her ability to blend humor and horror, further demonstrating her range.

Selena's television career has also been impressive, with starring roles in the hit series "Wizards of Waverly Place" (2007-2012) and "Only Murders in the Building" (2021-present). The latter has received critical acclaim and commercial success, with Selena serving as executive producer and star.

Throughout her career, Selena has demonstrated her ability to adapt to different genres, characters, and mediums. Her dedication to her craft and her willingness to take risks have made her a respected and beloved actress in Hollywood.

Exploring New Genres and Characters

Selena Gomez has consistently demonstrated her versatility as an actress by exploring new genres and characters throughout her career. One of the earliest examples of this was her transition from Disney Channel's "Wizards of Waverly Place" to the controversial film "Spring Breakers" (2012), directed by Harmony Korine. This move marked a significant departure from her wholesome Disney image, showcasing her ability to take on edgier roles.

In "Spring Breakers," Selena played Faith, a young woman who becomes embroiled in a world of crime and violence. The film's dark and provocative themes were a far cry from her previous work, and her performance received mixed reviews. However, it demonstrated her willingness to experiment with new genres and characters.

Selena's next project, "The Getaway" (2013), was an action-thriller that further showcased her ability to adapt to different genres. In the film, she played a young woman caught in the middle of a dangerous conspiracy, opposite Ethan Hawke. Although the film received mixed reviews, her performance was praised for its intensity and vulnerability.

In 2015, Selena starred in "The Revised Fundamentals of Caregiving," a Netflix film that explored themes of grief, trauma, and redemption. Her performance as a young woman with muscular dystrophy earned critical acclaim, with many praising her nuanced and empathetic portrayal.

Selena's role in "The Dead Don't Die" (2019) marked another significant departure from her previous work. The horror-comedy, directed by Jim Jarmusch, featured an ensemble cast, including Bill Murray and Adam Driver. Selena's performance as a zombie-obsessed teenager showcased her ability to blend humor and horror, further demonstrating her range.

Her most recent project, "Only Murders in the Building" (2021-present), has seen Selena take on a new genre: true-crime comedy. As executive producer and star, she plays a true-crime podcaster investigating a murder in her apartment building. The show's critical acclaim and commercial success have solidified her position as a talented actress capable of excelling in various genres.

Throughout her career, Selena has demonstrated a willingness to take risks and explore new genres and characters. Her dedication to her craft and her ability to adapt to different roles have made her a respected and beloved actress in Hollywood.

9

Public Image

Selena Gomez's public image has been a subject of interest for many years, with her evolution from a teenage Disney star to a mature and confident artist being a remarkable journey. Her public image has been shaped by various factors, including her music, films, social media presence, and personal life.

Initially, Selena's public image was that of a sweet and innocent teenager, thanks to her breakout role in "Wizards of Waverly Place." Her wholesome image was further solidified by her early music releases, such as "Kiss & Tell" and "A Year Without Rain." However, as she grew older, Selena began to explore more mature themes in her music and films, leading to a gradual shift in her public image.

With the release of her album "Stars Dance" in 2013, Selena's public image began to take on a more mature and edgy tone. Her music videos, such as "Come & Get It" and "Slow Down," showcased a more confident and sensual side of the star. This new image was further reinforced by her role in the controversial film "Spring Breakers," which marked a significant departure from her wholesome Disney image.

In the following years, Selena's public image continued to evolve, with her becoming more outspoken about her personal life and struggles. Her battle with lupus and mental health issues has been well-documented, and she has used her platform to raise awareness and support for related causes. This vulnerability has endeared her to fans and cemented her status as a role model for young women.

Selena's social media presence has also played a significant role in shaping her public image. With over 200 million followers on Instagram, she is one of the most followed celebrities on the platform. Her posts often showcase her personality, humor, and style, giving fans a glimpse into her personal life. Her influence on social media has been recognized by various brands, leading to numerous endorsement deals and collaborations.

Despite her fame and success, Selena has faced her fair share of challenges and controversies. Her highly publicized relationships and breakups have been subject to intense media scrutiny, and she has faced criticism for her perceived "party girl" image. However, she has consistently demonstrated her resilience and ability to bounce back from adversity.

In recent years, Selena's public image has become more refined and polished. Her role as an executive producer and star of "Only Murders in the Building" has showcased her versatility and talent, further solidifying her status as a respected artist. Her dedication to her craft, her vulnerability, and her commitment to using her platform for good have all contributed to a public image that is both authentic and inspiring.

Overall, Selena Gomez's public image has undergone significant transformations over the years, reflecting her growth and evolution as an artist and a person. Her ability to adapt and reinvent herself has made her a beloved and enduring figure in popular culture.

Managing Her Public Persona

Selena Gomez has demonstrated a remarkable ability to manage her public persona, navigating the complexities of fame with grace and poise. Her public persona is a carefully crafted blend of her authentic self, her artistic expression, and her commitment to using her platform for good.

One of the key aspects of Selena's public persona is her vulnerability. She has consistently shared her personal struggles, including her battles with lupus, mental health issues, and relationship challenges. This vulnerability has created a deep connection with her fans, who appreciate her honesty and authenticity. By sharing her struggles, Selena has also helped to reduce the stigma surrounding mental health and chronic illness.

Selena's public persona is also defined by her passion for her craft. She is dedicated to her music, films, and television shows, and her enthusiasm is evident in every project she takes on. Her love for her work is infectious, and her fans appreciate her commitment to excellence. Whether she's performing on stage, walking the red carpet, or promoting her latest project, Selena always exudes a sense of excitement and gratitude.

Philanthropy is another essential aspect of Selena's public persona. She is dedicated to using her platform to support important causes, including education, healthcare, and social justice. Her work with organizations like UNICEF, the Make-A-Wish Foundation, and the Ryan Seacrest Foundation has made a significant impact on the lives of countless individuals. Selena's commitment to giving back has inspired her fans to get involved and make a difference in their own communities.

Selena's public persona is also shaped by her sense of humor and playfulness.

Selena frequently utilizes online platforms to share humorous moments and insights, offering a glimpse into her lighthearted personality moments from her daily life, and her fans appreciate her ability to laugh at herself. Whether she's posting a silly selfie or sharing a hilarious story, Selena always seems to find the humor in any situation.

Of course, managing a public persona is not without its challenges. Selena has faced her fair share of scrutiny and criticism over the years, from her high-profile relationships to her perceived "party girl" image. However, she has consistently demonstrated her ability to rise above the noise and stay focused on her goals.

Selena Gomez's public persona is a carefully crafted blend of vulnerability, passion, philanthropy, and humor. She has managed to build a loyal fan base by being authentic, relatable, and committed to using her platform for good. As she continues to evolve and grow as an artist and a person, her public persona will undoubtedly continue to inspire and delight her fans around the world.

Dealing with Paparazzi and Media Scrutiny

Selena Gomez has been in the public eye for most of her life, and as a result, she has had to deal with her fair share of paparazzi and media scrutiny. The constant attention can be overwhelming and stressful, but Selena has learned to navigate the challenges with grace and poise.

One of the most significant challenges Selena faces is the constant pursuit of the paparazzi. Wherever she goes, she is surrounded by photographers and videographers, all vying for a shot or a scoop. This can be frustrating and invasive, especially when she is trying to enjoy some downtime or privacy. Selena has been known to take steps to avoid the paparazzi, such as using private entrances and exits, wearing disguises, and traveling with a security team.

Despite her best efforts, Selena is often subjected to intense media scrutiny. Her every move is analyzed and criticized, from her fashion choices to her relationships. The media has a tendency to sensationalize and exaggerate, often focusing on the most controversial or provocative aspects of her life. This can be hurtful and damaging, and Selena has spoken out about the negative impact the media can have on her mental health.

To cope with the stress and pressure of the paparazzi and media scrutiny, Selena has developed a few strategies. She prioritizes her mental health and well-being, taking time for self-care and seeking support from loved ones and professionals when needed. She also focuses on her work, using her platform to promote positivity and inspiration. By channeling her energy into creative pursuits and philanthropic efforts, Selena is able to rise above the noise and maintain a sense of purpose and fulfillment.

Selena has also learned to set boundaries and prioritize her privacy. She is selective about the projects she takes on and the events she attends, choosing opportunities that align with her values and goals. She is also mindful of her social media presence, using her platforms to share positive messages and connect with her fans, while also maintaining a level of privacy and security.

In addition to her personal strategies, Selena has also spoken out about the need for greater accountability and respect in the media. She has advocated for more responsible reporting practices and has supported efforts to protect celebrities' privacy and security. By using her platform to raise awareness and promote positive change, Selena is helping to create a more supportive and respectful environment for herself and her fellow celebrities.

Overall, Selena Gomez's experiences with paparazzi and media scrutiny have been challenging, but she has shown remarkable resilience and grace in the face of adversity. By prioritizing her mental health, setting boundaries, and advocating for positive change, Selena is able to navigate the challenges of fame with poise and confidence.

Embracing Her Authentic Self

Selena Gomez has undergone a remarkable journey of self-discovery and growth, learning to embrace her authentic self despite the challenges and pressures of the entertainment industry. This journey has been marked by a willingness to confront her insecurities, let go of perfectionism, and cultivate a deeper understanding of her values and passions.

One of the key aspects of Selena's journey has been her struggle with perfectionism. As a former Disney star, she was often held to unrealistic beauty and behavior standards, leading to a constant sense of self-doubt and criticism. However, as she grew older and gained more control over her career, Selena began to reject these unrealistic expectations and embrace her imperfections. She has spoken publicly about her struggles with body image, mental health, and relationships, using her platform to promote a more authentic and vulnerable representation of herself.

Selena's music has also played a significant role in her journey of self-discovery. Her earlier work was often focused on themes of love and relationships, but as she grew older, she began to explore more introspective and personal topics. Her album "Revival" (2015) marked a significant turning point in her career, featuring songs that addressed her struggles with anxiety, depression, and self-acceptance. Her subsequent albums, "Rare" (2020) and "My Mind & Me" (2022), have continued this trend, showcasing her growth and vulnerability as an artist.

In addition to her music, Selena has also used her platform to promote body positivity and self-acceptance. She has been open about her struggles with weight and body image, using her social media presence to share unedited and unretouched photos of herself. By embracing her natural beauty and rejecting unrealistic beauty standards, Selena has inspired countless young women to do the same.

Selena's commitment to mental health awareness has also been a significant aspect of her journey. She has been open about her struggles with anxiety and depression, using her platform to reduce stigma and promote resources for mental health support. Her documentary "My Mind & Me" (2022) offered a candid look into her mental health journey, showcasing her vulnerability and resilience.

Throughout her journey, Selena has surrounded herself with a supportive community of friends, family, and colleagues. She has been open about the importance of her relationships, particularly her friendship with Taylor Swift, and has used her platform to promote the value of female friendship and support.

Selena Gomez's journey of self-discovery and growth has been a remarkable one. By embracing her imperfections, rejecting unrealistic expectations, and cultivating a deeper understanding of her values and passions, Selena has become a powerful role model for young women around the world. Her commitment to authenticity, vulnerability, and mental health awareness has inspired countless fans and cemented her status as a beloved and respected artist.

10

Fan Engagement

Selena Gomez has consistently demonstrated a strong commitment to fan engagement, using her platform to connect with her audience and build a loyal community of supporters. Her approach to fan engagement is comprehensive, elaborate, and detailed, encompassing various aspects of her career and personal life.

One of the primary ways Selena engages with her fans is through social media. With over 200 million followers on Instagram, she uses the platform to share updates about her life, career, and personal struggles. Her posts often feature behind-the-scenes glimpses into her music videos, concerts, and other projects, as well as candid moments from her daily life. Selena also utilizes Instagram's features, such as Stories and Reels, to share more intimate and spontaneous content.

Selena's social media presence is notable for its authenticity and vulnerability. She frequently shares her thoughts and feelings about topics like mental health, body image, and relationships, using her platform to promote positivity and inspiration. Her fans appreciate her honesty and openness, which has helped to build a sense of trust and connection between Selena and her audience.

In addition to social media, Selena engages with her fans through her music and performances. Her concerts and music videos often feature interactive elements, such as crowd-surfing and fan participation. Selena also frequently meets with her fans at meet-and-greets and other events, taking the time to listen to their stories and share her own experiences.

Selena's fan engagement is also evident in her charitable work. She has supported various causes, including education, healthcare, and mental health awareness. Selena often uses her platform to raise awareness and funds for these causes, inspiring her fans to get involved and make a difference.

Furthermore, Selena has created a dedicated fan club, known as the "Selena Gomez Fan Club." This community provides a space for fans to connect with each other, share their love for Selena's music and message, and access exclusive content and experiences.

Selena's commitment to fan engagement has been recognized and celebrated by her fans and the entertainment industry alike. She has won numerous awards for her social media presence and fan engagement, including the "Most Popular Female Artist on Social Media" award at the 2020 iHeartRadio Music Awards.

Selena Gomez's approach to fan engagement is comprehensive, elaborate, and detailed. By using social media, music, performances, charitable work, and a dedicated fan club, Selena has built a loyal and supportive community of fans who appreciate her authenticity, vulnerability, and commitment to connection.

Connecting with Fans on Social Media

Selena Gomez has been a trailblazer in connecting with her fans on social media, using various platforms to share her life, music, and passions with her audience. Her approach to social media is comprehensive and detailed, encompassing multiple aspects of her online presence.

Selena's Instagram account is a prime example of her commitment to fan engagement. With over 200 million followers, she uses the platform to share updates about her life, career, and personal struggles. Her posts often feature behind-the-scenes glimpses into her music videos, concerts, and other projects, as well as candid moments from her daily life, such as selfies and stories.

She also shares inspirational quotes and messages promoting positivity and self-empowerment, sneak peeks into her fashion and beauty preferences, and personal stories and experiences, including her struggles with mental health and body image.

Selena also utilizes Instagram's features, such as Stories and Reels, to share quick moments from her day and create short, engaging videos showcasing her personality and creativity. She has also used IGTV to share longer, more in-depth content, like behind-the-scenes footage or exclusive interviews.

In addition to Instagram, Selena is active on other social media platforms, including Twitter, Facebook, and TikTok. On Twitter, she shares quick updates, thoughts, and opinions on various topics, while on Facebook, she posts longer updates, photos, and videos, as well as engaging with her fans through comments and messages. On TikTok, she creates short, fun videos showcasing her creativity and humor.

Selena's social media presence is notable for its authenticity, vulnerability, positivity, and engagement. She shares her genuine thoughts, feelings, and experiences, connecting with her fans on a deeper level. She openly discusses her struggles and imperfections, inspiring her fans to do the same. She promotes uplifting messages and inspiration, encouraging her fans to spread love and kindness. And she actively responds to comments and messages, fostering a sense of community and connection with her audience.

By using social media in this comprehensive and detailed way, Selena

Gomez has built a loyal and dedicated fan base, inspiring countless young people around the world.

Meeting Fans and Touring the World

Selena Gomez has always been dedicated to connecting with her fans, and one of the ways she does this is by meeting them in person and touring the world. Her meetings and tours are always highly anticipated and well-received by her devoted fan base.

Selena's meet-and-greets are a special opportunity for fans to meet their idol and share a personal moment with her. She has held meet-and-greets in various locations around the world, from concerts and festivals to special events and charity functions. During these meetings, Selena takes the time to talk to each fan, sign autographs, and take photos. She is known for being warm, kind, and genuinely interested in her fans' lives, making each meeting a memorable experience.

Selena's tours are also a testament to her dedication to her fans. She has embarked on several world tours, performing in countless cities and countries. Her concerts are always high-energy and visually stunning, featuring elaborate stage sets, costumes, and choreography. Selena performs a mix of her hit songs, old and new, and often includes special surprises and guest appearances. Her tours are a celebration of music, dance, and community, bringing fans together from all walks of life.

One of the most notable aspects of Selena's tours is her commitment to inclusivity and accessibility. She has made a conscious effort to ensure that her concerts are welcoming and inclusive spaces for all fans, regardless of their background, race, gender, or ability. She has partnered with organizations to provide accommodations for fans with disabilities and has used her platform to raise awareness and support for social justice causes.

Selena's tours have also been marked by special moments and surprises. She has been known to bring fans on stage, give impromptu performances, and even surprise fans with special gifts and experiences. Her tours are a testament to her passion for performing and her desire to create unforgettable experiences for her fans.

In addition to her concerts and meet-and-greets, Selena has also used her platform to support charitable causes and give back to her fans. She has partnered with various organizations to raise funds and awareness for issues such as mental health, education, and LGBTQ+ rights. She has also been known to surprise fans with special gifts and experiences, such as VIP tickets and backstage tours.

Overall, Selena Gomez's meetings and tours are a reflection of her dedication to her fans and her passion for music and performance. She has built a loyal and devoted fan base by being genuine, kind, and inclusive, and her live performances are a testament to her talent and generosity.

Inspiring and Empowering Her Audience

Selena Gomez has consistently used her platform to inspire and empower her audience, particularly young women and girls. Through her music, performances, and public appearances, she has promoted a message of self-acceptance, confidence, and resilience.

One of the ways Selena has inspired her audience is by sharing her personal struggles and experiences. She has been open about her battles with anxiety, depression, and body image issues, using her platform to raise awareness and reduce stigma around mental health. By sharing her story, Selena has shown her fans that they are not alone in their struggles and that it's okay to ask for help.

Selena's music has also been a source of inspiration for her audience. Her songs often focus on themes of empowerment, self-love, and inner strength. She has written about her own experiences with heartbreak, self-doubt, and personal growth, creating a sense of connection and relatability with her fans. Her music has been a soundtrack for many young people's journeys towards self-discovery and self-acceptance.

In addition to her music, Selena's performances and public appearances have been a testament to her commitment to inspiring and empowering her audience. She has used her platform to promote positivity and inclusivity, often incorporating messages of love and acceptance into her shows and speeches. Her performances are often high-energy and visually stunning, featuring elaborate stage sets and choreography that celebrate individuality and self-expression.

Selena has also been a role model for young women and girls, showing them that they can be strong, confident, and successful without sacrificing their values or integrity. She has used her platform to promote feminist values and challenge gender stereotypes, inspiring her fans to be their authentic selves and pursue their passions.

Furthermore, Selena has been involved in various philanthropic efforts, using her platform to support causes that align with her values and beliefs. She has worked with organizations that support mental health, education, and LGBTQ+ rights, inspiring her fans to get involved and make a difference in their own communities.

Overall, Selena Gomez has been a source of inspiration and empowerment for her audience, particularly young women and girls. Through her music, performances, and public appearances, she has promoted a message of self-acceptance, confidence, and resilience, inspiring her fans to be their best selves and make a positive impact in the world.

11

Personal Growth

Selena Gomez has undergone significant personal growth throughout her career, transforming from a teenage Disney star to a confident, empowered, and vulnerable woman. Her journey has been marked by self-discovery, introspection, and a willingness to confront her insecurities and imperfections.

One of the most notable aspects of Selena's personal growth has been her development of self-awareness. She has learned to acknowledge and accept her flaws, recognizing that they are an essential part of her humanity. This self-awareness has enabled her to be more authentic and honest in her music, performances, and public appearances, inspiring her fans to embrace their own imperfections.

Selena has also worked to cultivate emotional intelligence, learning to navigate her emotions and respond to challenging situations with greater resilience and wisdom. She has been open also she leverages her online presence to openly discuss her personal battles with anxiety and depression, aiming to normalize the conversation around mental wellness and encourage greater understanding and support.By sharing her experiences and insights, Selena has helped her fans develop greater emotional intelligence and seek support when needed.

Another significant aspect of Selena's personal growth has been her development of a stronger sense of purpose and direction. She has explored her passions and interests, discovering new ways to channel her creativity and energy. Selena has become more intentional about her career choices, selecting projects that align with her values and goals. This clarity of purpose has given her a greater sense of fulfillment and happiness.

Selena's personal growth has also been marked by a greater emphasis on self-care and wellness. She has prioritized her physical and mental health, recognizing that taking care of herself is essential to her overall well-being. Selena has been open about her struggles with body image and self-acceptance, using her platform to promote positive body image and self-love. By prioritizing self-care and wellness, Selena has become a more confident and empowered individual, inspiring her fans to do the same.

Furthermore, Selena has developed a greater sense of empathy and compassion, using her platform to support and uplift others. She has been involved in various philanthropic efforts, supporting causes that align with her values and beliefs. Selena has also been a source of support and guidance for her fans, offering words of encouragement and inspiration during difficult times.

Selena Gomez's personal growth has been a remarkable journey of self-discovery, introspection, and transformation. She has developed greater self-awareness, emotional intelligence, purpose, and empathy, inspiring her fans to do the same. Selena's willingness to confront her insecurities and imperfections has made her a more authentic and relatable role model, and her commitment to self-care and wellness has set a positive example for her audience.

Learning to Prioritize Self-Care

Selena Gomez has been open about her journey of learning to prioritize self-care, recognizing the importance of taking care of her physical, mental, and emotional well-being. This journey has been marked by a series of milestones, setbacks, and triumphs, as she has worked to develop healthy habits and strategies for managing stress and anxiety.

One of the earliest milestones in Selena's self-care journey was her realization that she needed to prioritize her mental health. After experiencing a series of anxiety attacks and panic episodes, she recognized that she needed to seek help and support. Selena began working with a therapist, who helped her develop coping strategies and techniques for managing her anxiety.

As Selena continued on her self-care journey, she began to prioritize her physical health. She started by making small changes to her diet and exercise routine, such as cutting back on processed foods and incorporating more fruits and vegetables into her meals. She also began exercising regularly, finding activities that she enjoyed, such as hiking and yoga.

In addition to her physical health, Selena also prioritized her emotional well-being. She began practicing mindfulness and meditation, finding that these activities helped her to feel more grounded and centered. She also started journaling, using writing as a way to process her emotions and reflect on her experiences.

Selena's self-care journey has not been without its setbacks. She has faced challenges and obstacles along the way, including the pressures of her career and the scrutiny of the media. However, she has remained committed to her self-care practice, recognizing that it is essential to her overall well-being.

Throughout her journey, Selena has learned several important lessons about self-care. She has learned that self-care is not selfish, but rather essential to living a happy and healthy life. She has also learned that self-care is not a one-size-fits-all approach, but rather a personalized practice that must be tailored to each individual's unique needs and preferences.

Selena's commitment to self-care has had a profound impact on her life and career. She has become more confident and resilient, better equipped to handle the challenges of the entertainment industry. She has also become a role model for her fans, inspiring them to prioritize their own self-care and well-being.

In conclusion, Selena Gomez's journey of learning to prioritize self-care has been a comprehensive and detailed process, marked by milestones, setbacks, and triumphs. She has learned the importance of taking care of her physical, mental, and emotional well-being, and has developed healthy habits and strategies for managing stress and anxiety. Selena's commitment to self-care has had a profound impact on her life and career, inspiring her fans to do the same.

Embracing Her Imperfections and Flaws

Selena Gomez has undergone a remarkable journey of self-acceptance and self-love, learning to embrace her imperfections and flaws as an integral part of her identity. This journey has been marked by a series of transformative experiences, epiphanies, and moments of vulnerability, as she has worked to break free from the constraints of societal expectations and embrace her true self.

One of the earliest moments in Selena's journey of self-acceptance was her realization that she didn't have to conform to the unrealistic beauty standards of the entertainment industry. She began to embrace her natural beauty, rejecting the pressure to conform to societal norms. Selena started to focus on her inner qualities, such as her kindness, empathy, and compassion, recognizing that these traits were far more valuable than physical appearance.

As Selena continued on her journey, she began to confront her insecurities and flaws, rather than trying to hide or deny them. She started to share her struggles with her fans, using her platform to promote authenticity and vulnerability. Selena opened up about her experiences with anxiety, depression, and body image issues, inspiring her fans to do the same.

Selena's willingness to embrace her imperfections has been a powerful source of inspiration for her fans. She has shown them that it's okay to be vulnerable, to make mistakes, and to be imperfect. By sharing her own struggles and flaws, Selena has created a safe space for her fans to do the same, fostering a sense of community and connection.

Selena's journey of self-acceptance has also been marked by a greater emphasis on self-care and self-compassion. She has learned to prioritize her own needs and well-being, recognizing that she can't pour from an empty cup. Selena has started to practice self-care rituals, such as meditation, yoga, and journaling, which have helped her to cultivate a greater sense of inner peace and self-love.

Furthermore, Selena has learned to reframe her flaws as strengths, recognizing that they are an integral part of her unique perspective and creativity. She has started to see her imperfections as a source of beauty and character, rather than something to be ashamed of. By reframing her flaws in this way, Selena has been able to tap into a deeper sense of confidence and self-acceptance.

Selena Gomez's journey of embracing her imperfections and flaws has been a comprehensive and detailed process, marked by moments of vulnerability, self-discovery, and transformation. She has learned to prioritize self-care, self-compassion, and authenticity, inspiring her fans to do the same. By embracing her imperfections, Selena has been able to tap into a deeper sense of inner peace, self-love, and confidence, becoming a powerful role model for her fans and she serves as a shining example of self-love and acceptance, inspiring others to embrace their individuality and find confidence in their own unique identity.

Finding Purpose and Meaning

Selena Gomez has been on a journey of self-discovery, searching for purpose and meaning in her life. She has explored various avenues, from her career to her personal relationships, seeking to find a sense of fulfillment and direction.

One of the ways Selena has found purpose and meaning is through her music. She has used her platform to share her story, inspire her fans, and promote positivity and self-empowerment. Her songs have become anthems for many, providing comfort, solace, and motivation. Selena's music has also allowed her to connect with her fans on a deeper level, creating a sense of community and belonging.

In addition to her music, Selena has found purpose and meaning through her acting career. She has taken on roles that challenge her and allow her to grow as an artist, including her portrayal of Rachel in the Netflix series "13 Reasons Why." Selena's acting skills have been widely acclaimed for their complexity and subtlety, showcasing her impressive adaptability and talent for bringing diverse characters to life on screen.

Selena has also found purpose and meaning through her philanthropic work. She has supported various causes, including mental health awareness, LGBTQ+ rights, and education. Selena has used her platform to raise awareness and funds for these causes, inspiring her fans to get involved and make a difference. Her philanthropic work has given her a sense of purpose and fulfillment, knowing that she is making a positive impact on the world.

Furthermore, Selena has found purpose and meaning through her personal relationships. She has surrounded herself with loved ones who support and encourage her, including her family and close friends. Selena's relationships have provided her with a sense of belonging and connection, helping her to feel grounded and secure.

Selena's journey of finding purpose and meaning has not been without its challenges. She has faced setbacks and obstacles, including the scrutiny of the media and the pressures of the entertainment industry. However, she has persevered, using these challenges as opportunities for growth and self-reflection.

Through her journey, Selena has learned valuable lessons about purpose and meaning. She has learned that purpose is not something that can be found overnight, but rather something that evolves over time. Selena has also learned that meaning can be found in the simplest things, such as spending time with loved ones or pursuing one's passions.

Selena Gomez's journey of finding purpose and meaning has been a comprehensive and detailed process, marked by exploration, growth, and self-discovery. She has found purpose and meaning through her music, acting career, philanthropic work, and personal relationships, inspiring her fans and making a positive impact on the world. Selena's journey serves as a reminder that purpose and meaning can be found in many ways, and that it is never too late to discover one's true purpose in life.

12

Legacy

Selena Gomez's legacy is a testament to her enduring impact on the entertainment industry and beyond. With a career spanning over two decades, she has left an indelible mark on the world of music, film, and philanthropy.

Musically, Selena's legacy is one of versatility and evolution. From her early days as a Disney star to her current status as a chart-topping artist, she has consistently pushed the boundaries of her sound and style. Her music has inspired countless fans around the world, and her influence can be heard in the work of many other artists.

As an actress, Selena's legacy is one of depth and nuance. She has brought complexity and emotion to her roles, whether in film or television. Both viewers and reviewers have been deeply impacted by her performances, leading to a slew of accolades and recognition, including several awards and nominations, in acknowledgment of her exceptional talent.

Philanthropically, Selena's legacy is one of compassion and dedication. She has used her platform to raise awareness and support for various causes, including mental health, LGBTQ+ rights, and education. Her tireless efforts have made a tangible difference in the lives of countless individuals and communities.

Selena's legacy also extends to her impact on social media and popular culture. With millions of followers across various platforms, she has used her influence to promote positivity, self-acceptance, and empowerment. Her presence has helped shape the online landscape, inspiring a new generation of young people to embrace their individuality and speak their truth.

Furthermore, Selena's legacy is marked by her resilience and perseverance. She has faced numerous challenges throughout her career, including scrutiny, criticism, and personal struggles. Yet, she has consistently emerged stronger and more determined, using her experiences to fuel her creativity and passion.

In the years to come, Selena's legacy will continue to inspire and influence new generations of artists, actors, and activists. Her music, films, and philanthropic work will remain a testament to her talent, dedication, and compassion. As a cultural icon and role model, Selena Gomez's legacy will endure, a shining example of the power of passion, hard work, and kindness.

Impact on the Entertainment Industry

Selena Gomez has had a profound impact on the entertainment industry, leaving a lasting legacy that extends far beyond her own career. Her influence can be seen in the many artists, actors, and musicians she has inspired, as well as the changes she has brought about in the industry itself.

One of the most significant ways in which Selena has impacted the entertainment industry is through her music. She has been a trailblazer for Latinx artists, paving the way for others to follow in her footsteps. Her success has shown that Latinx artists can achieve mainstream success without sacrificing their cultural identity or heritage. Her music has also inspired a new generation of young people to embrace their own cultural backgrounds and to celebrate their unique identities.

Selena's impact on the entertainment industry can also be seen in her acting career. She has been a role model for young women, showing them that they can be strong, independent, and successful in their own right. Her performances have inspired a new generation of young actresses, and her dedication to her craft has raised the bar for all actors.

In addition to her music and acting, Selena has also had a significant impact on the entertainment industry through her philanthropic work. She has used her platform to raise awareness and support for various causes, including mental health, LGBTQ+ rights, and education. Her tireless efforts have inspired a new generation of young people to get involved in their communities and to make a difference in the world.

Selena's impact on the entertainment industry can also be seen in the changes she has brought about in the way that women are represented in the media. She has been a vocal advocate for women's rights and has used her platform to challenge the objectification and sexualization of women in the media. Her influence has helped to create a more inclusive and equitable industry, where women are valued and respected for their talents and abilities.

Furthermore, Selena's impact on the entertainment industry can be seen in the way that she has used her platform to promote positivity and self-acceptance. She has been a role model for young people, showing them that they can be successful and happy without sacrificing their values or their sense of self. Her influence has helped to create a more positive and supportive industry, where artists and actors can feel valued and respected for who they are.

Selena Gomez's impact on the entertainment industry has been profound and far-reaching. She has inspired a new generation of artists, actors, and musicians, and has brought about significant changes in the way that women are represented in the media. Her influence has helped to create a more inclusive, equitable, and positive industry, and her legacy will continue to be felt for years to come.

Inspiring a Generation of Young Fans

Selena Gomez has been a beacon of inspiration for a generation of young fans, who have grown up admiring her talent, dedication, and passion. She has been a role model, showing them that with hard work and perseverance, they too can achieve their dreams.

Selena's music has been a soundtrack for many young people's lives, providing comfort, solace, and inspiration during difficult times. Her songs have addressed themes of self-empowerment, love, and resilience, resonating deeply with her young audience. Her music has also been a catalyst for self-expression and individuality, encouraging young people to embrace their unique qualities and celebrate their differences.

Selena's influence extends beyond her music, as she has used her platform to promote positivity, kindness, and acceptance. She has been a vocal advocate for mental health awareness, LGBTQ+ rights, and anti-bullying initiatives, inspiring her young fans to embrace these values and make a positive impact in their own communities.

Selena's connection with her fans has been genuine and authentic, as she has taken the time to engage with them on social media, at concerts, and through meet-and-greets. She has shown a genuine interest in their lives, listening to their stories and offering words of encouragement. This has created a sense of community and belonging among her fans, who feel seen, heard, and valued.

Selena's impact on her young fans has been profound, inspiring them to pursue their passions, embrace their individuality, and become confident, compassionate, and creative individuals. She has shown them that success is not just about achieving fame or fortune but about staying true to oneself and making a positive impact in the world.

Selena Gomez has been a shining star, inspiring a generation of young fans to be their best selves. Her music, message, and compassion have created a lasting impact, shaping the lives of countless young people and inspiring them to make a difference in the world.

Leaving a Lasting Legacy

Selena Gomez's legacy will be a lasting one, cemented in the hearts of her fans and the entertainment industry. Her impact on popular culture, music, film, and philanthropy will continue to inspire and influence future generations.

Selena's music legacy will be remembered for its versatility, creativity, and emotional depth. Her songs have resonated with fans from all walks of life, providing comfort, solace, and inspiration during difficult times. Her music has also been a catalyst for self-expression and individuality, encouraging fans to embrace their unique qualities and celebrate their differences.

In the entertainment industry, Selena's legacy will be marked by her trailblazing path for Latinx artists. She has paved the way for others to follow in her footsteps, showcasing the importance of representation and diversity in media. Her success has proven that Latinx artists can achieve mainstream success without sacrificing their cultural identity or heritage.

Selena's philanthropic work will also leave a lasting legacy, inspiring future generations to use their platforms for good. Her dedication to mental health awareness, LGBTQ+ rights, and education has made a tangible impact on the lives of countless individuals and communities. Her tireless efforts have raised awareness, reduced stigma, and inspired others to take action.

Moreover, Selena's legacy will be remembered for her kindness, compassion, and empathy. She has used her platform to promote positivity, self-acceptance, and self-love, inspiring fans to be their best selves. Her genuine connection with her audience has created a sense of community and belonging, fostering a supportive and inclusive environment.

In the years to come, Selena's legacy will continue to inspire new generations of artists, actors, and activists. Her music, films, and philanthropic work will remain a testament to her talent, dedication, and passion. As a cultural icon and role model, Selena Gomez's lasting legacy will be a shining example of the power of kindness, hard work, and determination.

13

Future Plans

Selena Gomez's future plans are a testament to her unwavering dedication to her craft, her passion for helping others, and her desire to continue inspiring her fans. In the years to come, she plans to:

Expand her music career, exploring new genres and collaborations that showcase her growth and versatility as an artist.

Continue acting in film and television, taking on roles that challenge her and allow her to bring complex characters to life.

Grow her philanthropic efforts, using her platform to raise awareness and support for mental health initiatives, LGBTQ+ rights, and education.

Launch new business ventures, including a clothing line and a production company, that reflect her values and creativity.

Write a book, sharing her story and insights with her fans and inspiring them to embrace their own journeys.

Embark on a world tour, performing in cities and countries she has never visited before and connecting with her fans in person.

Collaborate with other artists, producers, and writers on new projects that push the boundaries of music, film, and television.

Continue to use her social media platforms to promote positivity, self-acceptance, and self-love, inspiring her fans to be their best selves.

Support and mentor up-and-coming artists, sharing her knowledge and experience to help them navigate the entertainment industry.

Explore new technologies and platforms, using her influence to promote innovation and progress.

Selena Gomez's future plans are a reflection of her boundless energy, creativity, and dedication to her craft and her fans. As she continues to evolve and grow, she will remain a shining example of the power of passion, hard work, and kindness.

Upcoming Projects and Collaborations

Selena Gomez has a slew of exciting projects and collaborations in the works, showcasing her versatility and dedication to her craft. She is set to star in the upcoming TV series "Wizards Beyond Waverly Place," a sequel to her hit Disney Channel show "Wizards of Waverly Place," reprising her role as Alex Russo. Additionally, she will appear in the film "In the Shadow of the Mountain," a drama directed by Danny Moder, where she will play the lead role of Silvia Vasquez Lavado.

In the music realm, Gomez has been teasing a new collaboration with Colombian singer Rauw Alejandro, titled "Baila Conmigo." The two artists have been sharing snippets of the upcoming song on social media, generating significant buzz among fans. She has also been working on her fourth solo studio album, expected to drop later this year. Gomez has been sharing updates from the recording studio on her social media accounts, building anticipation for new music.

Gomez has also been announced as the executive producer of the documentary series "Invisible Hands," which delves into the lives of migrant workers in the United States. The series is currently in production and is expected to be released later this year. Through her production company, July Moon Productions, Gomez has several projects in development, including a film adaptation of the novel "Thirteen Reasons Why," in which she will produce and star.

Furthermore, Gomez will perform at the "We the People" concert in Los Angeles in August, celebrating the city's diversity alongside a diverse lineup of artists. With these projects and collaborations, Selena Gomez continues to demonstrate her creative range and commitment to inspiring her fans.

Continuing to Evolve and Grow

Selena Gomez's journey of continuous evolution and growth is a testament to her dedication to her craft, her passion for life, and her commitment to inspiring others. As she navigates the ever-changing landscape of the entertainment industry, she remains steadfast in her pursuit of artistic expression, personal development, and philanthropic endeavors.

Gomez's evolution as an artist is evident in her music, which has transformed from the bubblegum pop of her early days to the more mature, introspective sound of her recent releases. Her willingness to experiment with different genres, collaborate with diverse artists, and tackle complex themes has resulted in a body of work that is both critically acclaimed and beloved by her fans.

Her growth as an individual is equally impressive, as she has faced challenges, overcome obstacles, and emerged stronger and more resilient. Gomez has been open about her struggles with mental health, using her platform to raise awareness, reduce stigma, and inspire others to prioritize their well-being. Her commitment to self-care, self-love, and self-acceptance has made her a role model for young people everywhere.

Gomez's passion for philanthropy is another aspect of her growth, as she has used her platform to support various causes, including education, LGBTQ+ rights, and mental health initiatives. Her dedication to giving back has inspired countless fans to get involved in their own communities, making a positive impact on the world.

In addition to her artistic, personal, and philanthropic endeavors, Gomez has also been focused on her business ventures, launching her own production company, July Moon Productions, and partnering with various brands to create content, products, and experiences that align with her values and passions.

Through her continued evolution and growth, Selena Gomez has cemented her status as a beloved, respected, and inspiring figure in the entertainment industry. Her commitment to her craft, her passion for life, and her dedication to making a positive impact on the world have made her a role model for millions, and her impact will persist, leaving a lasting inheritance of inspiration that will continue to motivate and influence generations yet to come.

Looking to the future with hope.

As Selena Gomez looks to the future, she does so with a sense of hope and excitement. With a career spanning over two decades, she has established herself as a talented actress, singer, and philanthropist, and she shows no signs of slowing down.

In the entertainment industry, Gomez is eager to take on new challenges and explore different roles and genres. She is passionate about storytelling and is committed to using her platform to share stories that inspire, educate, and uplift. With several projects in development, including films, television shows, and documentaries, Gomez is poised to continue making a significant impact on the entertainment industry.

In addition to her professional pursuits, Gomez is also focused on her personal growth and well-being. She is committed to prioritizing her mental and physical health, and she is passionate about inspiring others to do the same. Through her platform, she hopes to continue raising awareness about important issues, such as mental health, self-acceptance, and body positivity.Gomez is also dedicated to her philanthropic work, and she is eager to continue making a positive impact on the world. She is passionate about supporting causes that align with her values, including education, LGBTQ+ rights, and mental health initiatives. Through her foundation, she hopes to continue providing resources and support to those in need.

As Gomez looks to the future, she is filled with hope and excitement. She is eager to continue growing, learning, and evolving, both personally and professionally. With her talent, passion, and dedication, she is sure to continue inspiring and making a positive impact on the world for years to come.Gomez's hope for the future is rooted in her belief in the power of kindness, compassion, and empathy. She hopes to continue spreading love and positivity, and she is committed to using her platform to make a difference. With her infectious smile, her generous spirit, and her tireless work ethic, Gomez is a shining example of what it means to live a life of purpose and meaning.

In the end, Selena Gomez's future is bright, and her potential is limitless. With her talent, passion, and dedication, she is sure to continue inspiring and making a positive impact on the world for years to come.

Conclusion

Selena Gomez's journey is a testament to the power of resilience, dedication, and passion. From her humble beginnings to her current status as a global superstar, she has consistently inspired and entertained audiences around the world. Through her music, films, and philanthropic work, she has left a lasting impact that goes far beyond.

With a career spanning over two decades, Selena Gomez has established herself as a talented actress, singer, and philanthropist. She has captivated audiences with her versatility, playing a wide range of roles in films and television shows, including "Wizards of Waverly Place," "Spring Breakers," and "The Fundamentals of Caring." Her music has also been a huge success, with hits like "Good for You," "Same Old Love," and "Lose You to Love Me."

But Selena Gomez's impact goes beyond the entertainment industry. She has been a vocal advocate for mental health awareness, LGBTQ+ rights, and education. She has used her platform to raise awareness and funds for various causes, including the Selena Gomez Fund for Mental Health, which she established in 2020.

Despite facing numerous challenges, including health issues and personal struggles, Selena Gomez has consistently demonstrated her strength and resilience. She has been open about her struggles with depression and anxiety, using her platform to reduce stigma and promote mental health awareness.

As she looks to the future, Selena Gomez continues to evolve and grow, pushing boundaries and exploring new horizons. Her commitment to her craft, her passion for life, and her dedication to making a positive impact on the world are a shining example for generations to come.

Selena Gomez's story is one of hope, inspiration, and triumph. She is a true icon and a beacon of light, shining brightly for all to see. Her legacy will continue to inspire and uplift, a reminder that with hard work, determination, and a passion for life, anything is possible. With her talent, passion, and dedication, Selena Gomez will undoubtedly continue to make a positive impact on the world for years to come.